AN ORGAN OF CHAOS

D.L. MARCUS

Copyright © D. L. Marcus, 2022

All rights reserved. The author asserts their moral rights in this work through the world without waiver. No part of this book may be reproduced, or stored in a retrieval system, or transmitted in any form or by any means, electronic, mechanical, photocopying, recording or otherwise without express written permission of the publisher.

For information about permission to reproduce selections from this book, write to: organofchaos@gmail.com

ISBN 978-1-925842-43-2 (paperback)

FIRST EDITION

Front artwork by author.

Photograph in Biographical Note by Brigitte Podrasky.

Joanne Fedler Media
Dolphin Street
Coogee
2034
Australia

www.joannefedler.com

For the part we try keep hidden
as it tries, in turn, to hide us

ORGAN-IC CONTENTS

EPILOGUE	7
?	9
CHORIC MEMBERS	
loot the salute	10
depression	11
when science names poetry	12
telling myself no	15
red dye	16
blood is grey	17
sweet disentanglement	18
do you write poems about Israel?	20
discomfort	21
and (stubborn) mirror rim DNA	22
(repeating reimagined revocalisations)	23
on rain-prisons, like liquid skin-mesh	24
inedible orchid	26
anxiety	28
a liquid rock that thinks	29
Blind Instinct	30
peppercorn vault	31
I am a Fractal	32
fucked like you meant it	34
avuncular unfamily	35
red blood cell beat	37
uncut	38
the paradox of layered line-loops	39
she is crazy	40

quadratic antiformula	41
varnish vanishing	42
sue the supine pine	43
sue me	44
why i hate sex	45
weak	46
I am writing as if I am a lie	47
grotesque tetris	49
love as missed mist-mystery	52
there is dialectic dust on my presence!	53
on beauteous dumbness	54
333	55
the beauty of loss	56
don't fucking call me jew	57
burning ship	58
scrollwork	62
I am only ready to make certain absolute statements	63
>> : a weak swimmer, necessarily filled with ocean	64
am I obsessed with loss?	66
window room	67
unknowing value	68
the nature of solids	69
a grotesque trifactor	70
hydrophobic	71
the Fleeting Features of Metric Feet and Metres	72
you: dendritric sub-type! sell your copyright!	74
the nature of copyright in nature	75
on trying to describe nature	76
perhaps I can ascribe beauty in technological terms	77
arbitrarily close	78

instruments like to be strummed	80
a bottle, on all fours, on all eights	81
plum wine	82
photo 51	83
Kevin Kookaburra	84
crude observation	85
fractal bulge	86
tricolonoscopy	87
decision becomes rampant	88
ACKNOWLEDGEMENTS	90
BIOGRAPHICAL NOTE	91

EPILOGUE

When I write, I approach death. Unless my words preserve and unconceal, I will remain inside a grave that nobody but me can see or feel.

It is a lonely being, being lonely inside a grave made of skin and organs and blood that everyone keeps telling you is alive, and you *know* is alive — but doesn't *feel* truly breathing. There just isn't enough air in my lungs: and this is why I write. There just isn't enough ground beneath my feet: and this is why I write. There just isn't enough vision inside my small, human eye: and this is why I write.

But I hate 'the why'. The question tries to make utility out of something I know is strictly anti-utility: seeking clear purpose in something that by definition lies in muddied waters or haze.

The art I love dances around meaning in circles of flame and ice, transforming every act of observance. Indeed the Truth has infinite faces, and is almost infinite in form. Hence it is logical that the Artist's appetite is infinite too, if Truth is the food fed naturally to the starving heart.

Yes — I write because I am starving. I have had many years of wakefulness, but I still do not yet feel awake. I have had thousands of dreams in the night, but none have yet satisfied me. I am still hungry, I am still searching.

One of my few certainties is that the heart is literate. Our hearts all contain complex stories of absolute chaos, pure bliss, and the nonsense-words that go with them, ringing. Our hearts can all write, if we allow a certain degree of chaos to reign. I have come to befriend this chaos. I can now see her as the pattern through which I grow; rather than that which ends me.

Sometimes, when I finish a poem — my blood effervescing, my internal voice as voltage — it glares back at me in haste. This poem, this damned Verbal Thing in front of me is the most Sudden, the most Complete Utterance that my Bloodied Heart e'er fucking saw.

It is my nonsense — and only my nonsense — that is so twisted and torn and clear and born that against all odds, against all sodden odds but one: it has let the light through!

A tiny, polished fleck.

I relish in these moments, as the semblance is always gone by morning.

Here then, I offer you these flecks.

My poetic organs.

D. L. Marcus

?

to be a Poet is to misunderstand
the understanding misunderstood

it is to be wrapped inside
an Ouroborotic romance
of solitude, of world-beginnings & ends
that do little to quell, dispelling
the ever-present Quiet

loot the salute

dissipative structures
lobular manifolds
these are the terms i am told
to be of value within
my other nonsense, babbling

depression

inauthentic-
ally myself

a slogan for the resonant
days, or dead-ended ways
they were afraid of you becoming

when science names poetry

a strange way, to iteratively
ruin the mood of the room
the poetic foot must not dare
step foot into the loot of the analytic

as remnant repenting
as roiled root, repeating
(you are, but silly, as poet)
you cannot be what is!
you are only like!
you are only as!

I am only. I am only.

a multitudinous sack of baloney
ham, sham, who gives a damn?
not me – I guarantee
"either-or" has never been clear to me

you see, to just call this thing "emergence"
to call it "iterative feedback"
is as ludicrous, is as sterile
as going over the dead grave
of my father with a burlap-sack of corn-starch
drizzling, like inedible shower
then commenting on how, the powdered flour-now
makes a sprinkle-coat on the then-green grass
that the grave-mower will precisely ignore at three

forty-two PM tomorrow
mowing-over it anyway, regardless of the measurement!

you see, to just call it a "strange loop"
is to look at a fingerprint – (the ones we all merry-well have) –
and to call it strange! as if the most regular part of it all
– our shared individuality – is an alien thing!

as if to have two eyes is mysterious, a hoot
as if to have two lungs is indescribable and rare

as if you, by being bilateral
but not-almost always bilateral
(one liver one pancreas one spleen one stomach
one heart that goes slightly asymmetric)
is strange! wow, let's reconnect the perverts together
with some invisible app, my dilution
is inevitable, as a poet
my denunciated delusion will settle
as meek-remark
as disregarded sentiment, I am anti-sediment
strangely un-alike the core that construes me!

the poet is like a poet!
the poet is as close to the poet as person can be!

but, oh, how (strangely), how (rose-grey tragically)
that the strange loop of self can be reduced
to some scope
of verbal figurative formula:

a dynamic feedback-based self-reflexively
self-entwined iterative recursive fractal feedback
based-system of complex multiplicity, oh, just put it simply!

to be simple is to be a mess
to be invisible, is to be comp-lex

telling myself no

repeated trauma is a warm,
drunken moth

fluttering sunkenly
toward the moon-bloodblood
of the soon-monsoon
misted grey, in the-midst of you

red dye

red diagonals
red bilaterals
red chromatical
red bihabital
red dialectical
red besplatical
red kinetical
red anorexical
red hypothetical
red forgettical
red connectical
red clavicle
red habital
red flammable
red shadow-full

red bets
red debts
red wets

blood is grey

looking up, again
beneath the sign
considered as benign
I am I am I am
I swear I have a power without
the will to know I am

a grey swatch that
when one looks closer
perchance not be it may

without fracture, I hope
my heart plummets the same
to remember, by the name
or, grab her skull
loose hair
wrung around around the body

suffocating the flesh
and with it become
fresher, less dense
within
embodiment
within

sweet disentanglement

my questions are eternal, inextricable
from the cables in my neck, the columnar
happening of impulse, i cannot recur
without repetition of known things, buzzing
along like demented bee, i try to recall
the gap i forged which let the light through

i am trying to let the light through
but it just comes and goes like tornado

without a neck my head would make more sense
without a head my body would make more sense

if i travel around the globe in search of the real
globe or sphere, reality becomes
a set of conditions where materials tend to react
react react react react react retract
in a particular way, our reality is just a certain
type of form, typing along increasingly
paralysed and analytic
axes axing
within the reductive lens of supposed absolutes,
i am morphologised and unable to become

something separated from fractal regressions
or repressions, it's the depression which
becomes a-central-mission, wondering weather
when you miss the

boat of truth along the
river of time whether the
weather-salesman will give you a refund
for such a dismantled thought

(such as finishing along, without knowledge
sitting on the-verge of the-ledge without mission)

when the construction of fruits is recognised
to be a poem: i will die, until then

do you write poems about Israel?

woah, are you really
a full-time poet?
Jewish huh!
I've never met a jew before!

discomfort

a hyperbolic pustule
permeating, perchance
my groin

picking apart your taste
moaning against
:
a stammer
a needle

and (stubborn) mirror rim DNA

as a worm-reflex on the skin I stiffen
to continue the natural disaster. naturally,
the disaster was me.

I tried to refrain from picking
a conscious pattern, but the departure
from normalcy was too threatening.

I like my rivers wide and worn like
how you left a stain on my shirt.

I couldn't get it off: no matter the thought,
no matter the soda, I just wanted to share
drunkenness with you. I don't even like drinking
hot, wet
disasters like you wouldn't have a clue
of the real weight of it
you haven't even lived yet kiddo
we will never be the same

can't I see?
I can't see...

(repeating reimagined revocalisations)

I have a voice inside
that would like me to die.

it's not a reason why
I *will* die
but it would like to try.

this voice
(that you have never heard)
is enough to make me absurd, freakish
and unburden myself upon you
so i am as light! as upon! a feather!

NO.
no weather I cause was ever inflicted
was ever inflicted upon you!

on rain-prisons, like liquid skin-mesh

the cold weather of my munching
heart is enough of a core-stricken
start to end the middle days I held

so close, clotting the curdled cut
I can't believe the plot
the way a cigarette
is mostly forsaken, forgotten

I am thing
I am this: thinking
blood, it's flesh and bone
the misgiving of living in the same home:
refusing, rediffusing; ending-up inside-the-carpet
synonymous with surfaces

to recall the endeavour
was something alike differentiation
or the inner station, whatever was morose, the gore-worm
is a-good-enough title for me

though it ought to be a trickle,
a tickle or a tap of two
to know — (it always was and will be) — me-right-over you

(I say this, alarming and uncold)
(I say this, knowing words untold)

like will you ever forgo forgiveness
for my obsession with disease?

I know it doesn't come easy or
it merely comes alongside a body
fraught with pores or

porcelain misunderstandings
of the nature of crime and time

inedible orchid

unlearnable ballads circulate
around around the skull, sulking
in the dead-car, in the dead-night
wishing against tomorrow

the wake is a fright
the face is a sight
that makes me want to de-skin

how else to form
the sense of deep

vulnerable facets
coming-to fruition

like when I spend the train ride
as an insane passenger passing

thinking thinking thinking makeup
would transform your decision-but
it was only my silhouette you saw

I am a baby-toothed child
inside my eyes, inside my panoptic
vision of myself, the way a lady-slipper orchid
dies and tries again
locked inside a jar, a dried rot

I am nothing but a tired slot
into which air and calories feed

I don't know how to say I had just
been looking been looking
to have someone I trust to love

anxiety

pulsing, mid-
on the mind-floor
wait! I will join you there:
and you! and you! and you!

a liquid rock that thinks

perched atop a hard, historical thought
I wonder why

(I may not know what I am
but I know I am
not as hard as you
I know neither of us
a rock
so why be solid?)

you tell me, immediately
to be hard is the only way!
it's the only way to be!

(despite, and notwithstanding
the reality
of amniotically)

Blind Instinct

/// M-Eye Instinct has no Eyes, only I's launching /// Multifaceted Swings of Be coming /// This-That or the Other /// "I am Afraid of your-Becoming /// another-I /// without any Eyes or I's I remember! !!" /// do you have a memory of the first amniotic thought? /// (.it was microscopic.) /// (only Men will say that They Remember!) /// /// (the thought   Blind or T aught – /// Imprisoned just-for Caring); / /// /// or for patterns, all. four. blinks! //

peppercorn vault

it was all her fault

motivated by my own disappearance motivated by

the so-called-empathetic

thought of you mentally

betraying me the thought of my shape

as nuisance holds strong despite

you being inflated, despite my own

deflation of self that betrays

the real me, I am larger than

I am I am not what I am not, I am not what I knot as knotted

entrails trailing down the beds waking shaking cold

red as I am said, mirror-told

raiding, fading

I cannot help but sense the fading

her pattern as something undealt, concealed, dispersed:

was her end into ocean?

I cannot help but presume

not commun-icative my voice but-box

box-because someone assaulted it, locks

and i keep telling myself that I let him

I am a Fractal

circle in the centre, circle in the centre of the centre
I twist and envelop the former; I am eating the bend
regurgitating as a fold, I stretch and develop
into a band of concentric recursion
pink forgetting, in mottled patches

if I stare at the patch for long enough it throbs

it is the same throbbing recursion that prevents sleep
dries my neural nodes and leads to the same
concentric regurgitation
the enveloping appetite
of my cognition that speeds as a double
thought in thoughts
edges that join into a corner of another's edge

I am a wedge as a tip of a point into another tipped point
shadows behind the tree; the breeze unfolds, into my limbs,
into the limbs of others

branching as a separation, I join into your folds
and find the liberty of regression as an infinite thing

as my colour changes and shape holds, I find another shadow
behind the original shape, there is a new corner I had not foreseen

the rivulets are embedded with grease and microbes, I harbour
more than the boundaries of self; engrained in my surface politics
are the recursions of others; trying to find
the resemblance in the semblance

concentric gatherings as unfolding into squares
locked, into a corner, and bashing the apertures into formation

into complicity I code my becomings, into concentricity I admit:
folding and unfolding as a riverbed
and as a reflection, I hold

fucked like you meant it

why is my poetic
pulse-led
by urgencies of repletion?

why is my gymnastic
mind minding
only the lacks, tending to the ledge as I edge
against the shallow fold traipsing?

I want to be engulfed by you entirely! and properly—
not by you engulfing your vision of an image
you obtained of me, only by forgetting!

what????
what did I forget?!
you forgot to question, piece of shit!
to beget or fuck me!

you got too comfortable in the mould so it
grew mould and now we're stuck-within
another empty,
lurking pattern

avuncular unfamily

I hate to say I'm hatred
but loving seems unfit

battling, from the parapet
but I don't want to convince

thoughts, of being pet-food
you, remaining unmoved

beyond the howl of hours
you allocated to running

from grief (it seems, always)
to be working, you say

you seem to be working away
from a central-thing in vision

red-circle, crimson rope
but don't allow the settlement

to grope against divorce
but don't allow the sediment

to crisp, darken and bloat
into inedible callous because

we are taught not to glisten!
against listening devices

unless—within crisis—to hold
against the division's remain

I swear
I'm true

as a never-blue substance
returning, just like sub-uncle

red blood cell beat

```
                    BLOODBLOODBLOOD
                  BLOODBLOOD   BLOODBLOOD
                BLOOD   BLOOD   BLOOD   BLOOD
             BLO   OD   BLO   OD   BLO   OD   BLO   OD
         BL   O   O   D   BL   O   O   D   BL   O   O   D   BL   O   O   D
      B   L   O   O   D   B   L   O   O   D   B   L   O   O   D   B   L   O   O   D
         BL   O   O   D   BL   O   O   D   BL   O   O   D   BL   O   O   D
             BLO   OD   BLO   OD   BLO   OD   BLO   OD
                BLOOD   BLOOD   BLOOD   BLOOD
                  BLOODBLOOD   BLOODBLOOD
                    BLOODBLOODBLOOD
```

uncut

to be a poet is to be incomplete, to bulge
with inexpressibility
yet told by all
others to be enunciated and precise
in some vague, unspoken way

hurray!
I have simply been misunderstood,
unencompassed, yet again.

the paradox of layered line-loops

interference patterns, moiré effect
fancy terms for my underlying regret
of not having words to explain my vision
of not having words to explain my song

here I am: drifting along
too cold to say I care
too old to say I am no longer a child

what? being mildly
inclined toward the mirror is something
being mildly swine-like is enough to forge genocide
against dissimilarity, yes?

I am a mere paradox!
of layered line-loops

trying to remember
why I chose to forget

she is crazy

she is crazy for being
a circle she is crazy just-for
being-she is crazy for becoming
aloof: aloof: a loop.

quadratic antiformula

erect tangle
disallowed cows
perched on-the-street

don't hackle, my ask
it is meek.

varnish vanishing

as lacquer, as gloss
I tarnish on the flood-door
of the mind-floor, fumbling
like a kitten or an image

smitten in the darkness
while high, off-allergic
detergent used to repel
the opposite
the facts
so don't be slack or slick

like messy oil, non-essential mesh
like a biiiiiiiiiiiiiiiig oil slick on your back baby!

as a crater I forsake her and wonder r r r r r r r
lolling my prehistoric tongue
like frozen bile

but the chaos is pre-emerging, rolling
like I know how to know knowing now

sue the supine pine

for it is weak—backless,
the withdrawn
location of many dendritic
membranes reconcealing
the failed forgettance
of shoulders,
the angular, eloping—always bound but-to hoping
the short-wound-around the short, reduced spines
of leaves-reduced to frilling
joint segments

sue me

maybe I'm ovulating, or maybe the ellipse is just a natural thing
to have ovals within me, fizzing
like the demented grey I see about you
at my lowest, when I
just want
to be held, by any figment especially

(all you men are just symbolic!
figure-heads from who I want head.

at least — this is what I think the people think of me
who are growing tired or scared trying to read me.

but they don't really know
how if I give head I just
I lose the mystery tension rope
I just suffoc-

eight. lips. shutting. tight.
hoping the silence into wide-open baby!
just to keep myself in the running
of always being forgotten
for a different reason,
season
or change
)

why i hate sex

when I am dried and dreaming
on the mind-floor, no recovered
thoughts muster the energy to flank
on the sides of the embankment, fleeing
so readily pursued as amusement
i increase the flagella and wonder
why my insides were the most valuable
transaction i could offer you, what caused
the deterioration of your care for knowing
me deeper, for you simply felt the depth
with appendages, instead

weak

the search of melody
becomes malady, my lady

I swear my taste for tradies came
at the cost of realising I am not wood
so the carpenter is not able to reform
me into re-beginning

whenever I search
for the yellow I see it
in the butter-sky after
I see it in the decay

I always feel
the recoil but
don't worry about me—
she's strong!

I am writing as if I am a lie

no, not that kind of line
you silly little duck!
better get that gravel unstuck, you sticky sticky shoe
do you want to lick it (I don't mind) I kindajustwant
you to I don't mind the lie, if you do?   just

I'mkindamaybe just waiting for the kindamaybejustt
justification or reason to lead UUU into a slight-grey
that isn't the fleck from yourhead,, I do like it though
I promise I will vomit within the pace you set, I frolic
through the paths IU set out myself and dream about
and it's kinda maybe just U waiting for the right time
for it to be the wrong Utime, for time to make thebad
decision, it will always be a lucid choice when I chose
to dream of UUU subconsciously, lucid Umind dilute
pollute, restrained with the concrete thought of UUU
abstract, tantalizing as a metal bracket around ankles
secured to the throat,, I want to be a moat around UU
UU never-swim you never letme,, you only sink or die

will UU be killing yourself if IU ever become a love-lie?
it will just be a perversion IIIUUU, it will not be trueU,
I know what it is not to love and in not loving UU now,
& in not loving UU know, I will know I am notyetblind,
whenIsaythis, when I weigh U on cracked mechanisms,
but why does it feel so blinding to know III'll *** 4UUU
&& **** the bed && UU'll just lick it? I know it'd begold
&& not grey, I know I don't know how to know, that it'd

be sweet and grey, I want UUU to eat me like adeadrose
I want to be rotten, I am dying, IamUURsdying & it's all
because of the colour grey! I am notaUUcolour, I am not
thing that doesn't havefeelings, apparently III look to be
asexualperson, if only the generalpopulous knew theway
onetimesomeonehurtme and I have been hurt ever since
how the UIC is the U I need and I bleed 4 U, so U fuckin'
O me! kinda-like-playing-chess-but-the-squares-all-have
principlesofequitygoverningtheirvalueandit'sjustlikethis:

a grey board,
a grey player
and death awaits as rescuer

grotesque tetris

as a vision I banned
grotesque tetris, the becoming
of the interpersonal, transpersonal membrane

insane, dangerous
lurked onto-the-edge-of-us
the stickiness, the fumbling
always seems to be tumbling
along the edge or sense of sanity

along the other bilipid, I dance
along the insipid edge of chance:

how I am embedded within
a guttural sense of vision
a guttural sense of clarity

although, without; although-within,
the guttural sense of imagery
without, (although, within!)
the least-common set of them all.

I am just hot and lurking
I am just not and bursting
as I knot the not-knotted
entrails and swallow because
good girls ingest!

never in jest, though
never with vitreous humour
only within the virtue of future,
of entanglings I lurk

only within the future of bespangling I jerk
into the vision of a fixed clearance
into or as an aisle of discount
I swear I am
a swearing of I am a discounted, demented consumption!

so, so, so!
you consume me for a low price: the price of a shit microscope,
some coloured pencils, and a dead butterfly

so, so, no!
I will ask you to consume me, to give advice
on how to be whole, on how to fix holes
that comprise my soul, that you didn't cause but
you did largen them, you did commit enlargening

so, now, I am bargaining
to return to the un-pierced state:
the fabric of my woven dynamics
the fabric of my cloven jew-hooves

thirteen exact degrees in the direction
perpendicular to the horizon!
I am but a simple, changing salt!

so, when I salt the fabric of my words
with poetry, as a flavour
as a self-negating yet entangling favour
as a condiment,
a self-fragmenting continent
I am only
endearing, I am only grotesque
in clearings of my tasting
my own ingested gustation
as a discounted, clearance-vision
of rancid meat meeting
the other! oh, bother!

I merely assault the fabric
of my self when I commit poetry!

it is merely against my whole soul!
when I take the whole, the entire backseat
of the memory of the memory of the memory—

love as missed mist-mystery

to look at beauty with the face of god, I am
looking at the kiss, the missing
signals of her sighing
thigh, blatantly.

a dispersion of fluidity remakes the model
as a systematic endeavour I recover
dissipation
as an enamoured thing

singing on the toilet
and my mother can hear me!
I am sitting on the pond-pit and wondering how crepe
myrtles manage to sing so deeply, for so long?

how the rustle of their magenta curls
crisp within the wind-beat, how they are endowed
with the little, miniscule bits:

the time-boats
of the soul-mist particles
that the loved leave behind

there is dialectic dust on my presence!

an illustrious remark,
anti-disgust!

I am pressed-within dispersions-against
dialectic re-incursions
of spatiation I am trying to disperse-without
investigative instantiation,
but no matter the thought the space
still comprises
of two things:

the negative absence, the positive being
simple positivity, simple voids

(though the thought must be some hypercoin
because the artwork is dead with blinded
observers wiping, blowing off the blinding
dusts of the curling
vision, reduced to statistical remark)

on beauteous dumbness

you, dear:
I am attacking solely you
on you: who does not grovel
on you, who does not hope

333

it would be a small joke
to have a balloon as a body
(so God said, creating man

it would be a small joke to whisper
between trees, like the ones neatly
arranged, in threes)

the beauty of loss

holding in my hand, a shiny gloss
I will make a single dewdrop, an Escher-encapsulation
or organ:

(can you not see anything
except your own blooded distortion?!)

don't fucking call me jew

the word can only come from Our mouth
without implying Our death

I'm being serious
why do I have to tell you
I am being serious?

burning ship

even as a historical collection of dead jews
DEAD jews DEAD jews DEAD jews DEAD
dead-DAD JEWS dead DAD-JEWS dead
DAD. GAS. JEWS. BURNING. SHIP FUCKING BURNING
FRACTAL OF INFINITE FUCKING DEAD
JEWS DEAD DAD GAS BREA—

JEWS

DEAD JEWS

where is the why is the where is the why is the
dead bodies in piles plus dead bodies in piles plus
dead bodies in piles plus dead bodies in piles plus
dead bodies in piles dead bodies plus-frozen over
dead bodies in piles this is your GRANDMOTHER
soft-face gone-hard with MURDER. MURDER. MURDER.
dead bodies in piles your BROTHER dead his body
like rancid dog-treat, some dog meat around ribs

face-purple eyes-lost within his dead this-is more-than
death when the CHILD is shot for her jew-plot, a jew
CHILD CHILD CHILD CHILD C H I   L   D
KILL THE JEW-CHILD KILL THE SPAWN G A S G A S   S   S G A SS   SS SS
SS SS SS SS SS SS SS SS SS SS SS SS SS SS SS SS
SS SS SS SS SS SS SS SS SS SS SS ss ss s s s s s s s—
thump.

the FATHER is dead. it hasn't been a century.
but but but the people already twist, the people already ask
why is it that the jews get to decide what antisemitism is
why is it that the jews disagree about what antisemitism is
why is it that jews do not agree with me and some have money
why is it that the jews weaponise antisemitism against
non-jews, I will never have single answer to any extremist question
but I do know that memories are remembered and repressions
hit like concrete at-the-bottom of a collective grave holding
the dead-jew FRIEND you made last week, but always kept quiet

59

because why is it relevant to be outwardly pro-semitic in this age our death spreads heavy into history how death spreads death heavy like the nazi raping our skeletons some of them would still even be warm in the cold wet warmth of clotting blood gas gas suffocate can-I-hug your dead body so many times dead bodies timesed by dead bodies in piles-dead bodies in piles they buried your MOTHER's dead face like they are all being buried now now theburdentoothick.thick. like dead bodies in piles plus dead bodies in piles plus dead bodies in piles like sick fucking flesh mountains running off the cliff-face push your friend you both would be dead bodies in piles chasing-death up the blood-stairs anyway while the soldiers laugh: the humor of the dead jew buried like a secret they are buried as conspiracy for their own conspiracy. what am I meant to do when I can't where is the why is the where is the why is the see is the where is the why is the where is the why is he a BUTCHER laughing at the death of long-nosed rats

he doesn't sell meat doesn't buy meat he just freezes
the rancid meat of rancid whites or plague of RATS
too thick pushed into the crevice of photos deepbeneath
Berlin's streets the city's Holocaust museum lodged
under Berlin's streets the statues representing dead
graves dead bodies dead dead bodies dead people
just smoking cigarettes on them now they smoke
on the statue representing the dead bodies the piles
the smoke the bodies the dead: the dead dead jews

scrollwork

can I get this please
but no worries if not
I was just wondering if
no problem at all
I don't know
I tend to say the wrong things

I tend to I tend to
the edge of the ledge as I pledge
the duty of poet as edge
fighting as
no problem at all
I don't know
I was just wondering if
I could be
no problem at all
but no worries if not
I was just
I don't know
tending to the edge
I am
no problem at all
to wonder if I could please just get
the wrong things
I tend to please
alone and with
no problem, at all

I am only ready to make certain absolute statements

there, that is it

>> : a weak swimmer, necessarily filled with ocean

free forms playing
inside natural nests
don't feel like home

capture the morph
of the Mobius
as it sorts anaemic
amoeba

in the mornings I unfurl
curl against, tucking
into the nest-
led structure of vessels
my vessel

who snuck inside, looped
as I tried to tuck the freshest flesh
within-itself with-out my self
or truncated lies

the conditioned premonition
of the fallacy dripping
as a deadened throb

each slit diagonal
bilateral mirroring

so-vision is clarified as known
to be dripping
as the stifled wave-point drop
of netted sight
that falls-in to catch the answer

or death-wink drums
hide-stretching-over to be played
as a glass-struck harp before
the angel in the angle withdrew

why doesn't the tilt
making synthesis visible
offer knowing in the way
I thought it would

being able to see
the way the seas-lie-within
indeed makes a stranger
bigger than the absent
figure
I try gather >>

am I obsessed with loss?

looking back, I do retract
the statement I issued as true
I am somehow, now, looking down

always ridiculously impersonal, always ridiculously
paradoxical in my supposed suppositories

it is somehow
historically subliminal, divisional, in tact
to somehow, never-always, look back

window room

if the floor is a window
if the roof is a window

is the wall-window the same?
category, please! I need distinct

separations, anxieties, calamities!

unknowing value

prepositionally within the position,
assumed to be languid or, prophetically true

i rediscover myself within you, only to be
aware-now that it's a busy lie, tied into
the runaway vision of models, simulated
within a pixel-slime that cannot be seen or stroked
into the solitary wake, for goodness sake!
your level is not my colour!

the nature of solids

sometimes. when the stirring
is still enough
to be recorded
it is white hot.

liquid bricks, condensed
spilling, pressed

(if a fluid-house

construed
from my mirror
is hyperbolic,
perchance
I am
)

a grotesque trifactor

subliminally intact, I am urged
to be exact, within a bend
within the book-ends
of a reptilian-ruler
the central sphere is posited

as lobular, within fins of finished
burglary, the motor-control
of mycellic rhizomes
of blatantly becoming
or, blanketing the mirror
with-a-vision of fresh fish, and other scales
that were never made to measure
the tail-end of things

I am only left ringing
as a demented bell, I am
loops of repeated dementia
that pile, without dimension
beyond the Euclidian scope
of leisure,
beyond the purity
of Platonic pleasure

hydrophobic

rhizomes are liquid inside
)sorry, I had to tell you
before someone, (called me!)
would sew my mouth right-shut(

sight-against the winter pattern
I rust, I rusted, I had to tell you
how I almost burned my organs with frost, how I
I knew someone once, who would dream of slitting
throats inside the disease library
I saw, I have to tell you
the remnant of suicide,
from self-inflicted tracheal
slitting, or jumping
//
sitting inside the liquid
we all sit, I have to tell
someone about this, before it's all too late

it's too late but I have to ask, to ask you
dear-footed Person, without invisible acronym
within the bounds of invisible metric
feet, skidding along pounds
of sleet, will you coddle
the curdled cluster i begged of you?

for i am nothing but a livid
a used, liquid lipid – i am nothing but a cyst!

the Fleeting Features of Metric Feet and Metres

lignified, by arctic grasses
by the liberty denied
by the minute-mute minutes.

Life As Death's Overside!
is equivalent in valency
to Penrose's illusions to the Poet

(Infinity is a twisted braid
made to ponder)

&

so while I am
wondering about the invisible drips
in the membrane's shape;
in the same way you drive along
a road and there's a big hill you can't see the drip
behind the hill
doesn't mean the drop
is not there just because-you
are twisted into a concrete system
of empirical forces, enforced by Empires
that lie to the mundane colours
of the lyrebird, & refuse to tell the truth that they can tell us

I am just looking inside of nothing
I am just looking inside of nothing: inside my brain

the way an inside-look into the inside poet
dispels the illusions, yet confirms, that they are insane

is that not the thing to gain?
am I not the thing to gain when The Law frames laws as
something akin to not-being-able-to-plagiarise-the-poet
because you Cannot Plagiarise Sentiment?

what is meant by being
if I can muster the full intensity
of certain word pairings yet fail
to muster contemporaneous
cognition, the experience of being needed

for the feelings that I feel synonymously
as Private; as Professional?

Tell Me! who or what will save us
when the ones who can forge
new meaning from language
have all suicided or coincided
into neater;
weaker, advertised copies?

you: dendritric sub-type! sell your copyright!

the law of the tree is serious
people like to laugh when confronted
with their reliance on their own trees

you are part-tree, at absolute minimum:
your lungs are filled with trees. your blood-tree
finds every cell between
the plasmic discordance comprising
the fluid-channels directed by your heart

(although, somehow, not an art
in the eyes of the entrepreneur looking to make a quick-buck
completely ignorant of the seriousness
of Poetics)

the nature of copyright in nature

mimesis; in short
(if you want a long answer
or more explanation
you will have to stay here for awhile
and not look for the symbol's answer)

on trying to describe nature

metalanguage makes me unhinged
from my seat
embarrassingly bare
to the user, in my movement.

you can sense my confusion at the prompt
if I have to re-shell the question
within its own encasement.

perhaps I can ascribe beauty in technological terms

certainly, if I called my child this title
I would be deemed as ridiculous mother

yet people get away with monosyllabic
or tongue-twist curses, daily,
that have no clickity-clack to ascribe-back regardless!

look at the state of the vine twisting against its spine
against my curtains (I lie—it's against the wall—)

perhaps it makes sense, the difficulty, that is
to recall
to recall

arbitrarily close

again, like the two butterflies
we began an encounter not dissimilar
to a murmurance deathly repeated

becoming an unspoken
trauma by me,
and a subconscious, by you.

I will tell myself it's unconscious by you
i know it's not
i just don't have the means
to imagine you imagining her—
the way she (your-old-her) has been constructed
for me, is something like a bad dream.

when i am just given the end
when we are just given
the end
it changes the taste
the pace of beginning

i try to not remember the shell
the narcissist man (before you) made of me
or the shell the mechanic pummelled me into
(before that) or the shell I pummelled myself into (before
him) or the shell my dad vacated (before it all)

the narcissist is the hardest to remember.
i was justabout ready to stay with a man
who split me away from my friends, my family
who liked to guilt me into sex, cry when I became upset
tell me my worries for his safety made him want to actually kill himself
say I'm almost finished when I asked him to stop fucking me

say there was actually a silver-lining
to him drunkenly fucking his best friend
the week before my mother was getting cancer surgery

say four years meant something: anything at all
yet refuse to pick up the phone after cheating
or ever see me again

if I gave this stranger an expensive textbook back
explained to him the reason why I kept calling
he texted he would consider picking up the phone
in the "medium-distant future"

the city's first lockdown began that week
the only other time i have felt this alone was wailing
inside a psychiatric
ward at night, wishing death

somehow, he must have gotten off on it
deprioritising my being, that is
until i had nothing to become, except his

instruments like to be strummed

so, by virtue
of the inner resonance:

consumption will be summed
discounts will be counted
space, will be aced
flowers will owe
flasks will ask
mothers will other
flies will lie
insides will side
and humans like to be manned!

(manhandled, I am told
is a subtle, unkind thing
but not to worry, the shadow
will always
h
h
hold)

a bottle, on all fours, on all eights

even when standing, my soul likes to sit
do I have a lazy soul, the age-old
question told, the notion of self-preservation
as marmalade, I am lying on my body
as if it is manna, in the manner-of-thought
hydrated, within a branching spectrum
of descent, of lentils, of fruit

plum wine

within the brief history of fruits
a structure is reduced:
small, plum-like
a stone within-the-middle

how curious! to be encoded
as carrying a crop or core
that can be reconstrued, resoftened
for fractal, regressive purpose

photo 51

a doctor trap
on war-DNA

was part raw,
part eye-DNA

(and eye-trap war-trap saw

and raw,
no part-rot coda)

Kevin Kookaburra

when I am leaving spaces early
when I am looking into nothing
with the look of nothing
on my face, in my eyes
it's because of you
it's because of you

when I hear the echo
of the death-membrane
when I sit inside the sun
feel the coldness

that has not yet arrived
that I am not yet feeling
but it's inside your sin
but it's inside my skin

when I'm learning
from myself, and not from you
it's because of you
it's because of you

crude observation

quickly, (almost-as-if
a new thought, she noticed

to be a Poet was to be
trapped-within a dialectical wrapping
of herself, of-sorts)

fractal bulge

I saw a tree that gave
me the answer it gave

generously I looked away
for a glimpse is already the largest
grasp of the infinite

tricolonoscopy

I have a little printed copy of my inside-organs
with real outside-photos, the replica of the inner
that I am always hungry-for.

alas, what do you do when you are but an organ
relying on the dissective consumption of its own
tissue as a means of fulfillment?

when vision is autoimmune—
when eyeball has tongue?

decision becomes rampant

to funnel inside-of the dream
time-space bends within
a honeycombed twist of axiom
into hyperbola twisted
into hyperbole

a single pixel
a single rounding
foreshadowing, sounding
akin to lukewarm
juxtaposition, a single decision

emblematic of turgidity
my problems porously sweat

am I simply an emblem
or problem to forget?

reduced to insane-insignia,
the way I is experienced?

I, as an idiom for X-marks the spot?
I, as an idiot for the mark-marking between us?

yes.
you are *that*: that which singularises the multiplicious
you! becoming symptom
for everything that I hate

such as, the weakness of memory
in-morning, such as, the weakness of voice
underfoot
the weakness of throats twinning

like twine around my spine,
spinning around my twin
vertically as vertebrae
certifying my cerebral
mutterings that never-mattered
to anything but you

but they do matter.
I. Does. Matter.

like a twist, like a sweet, sick vibration
inside, into bliss
inside, contemplation
the collateral decision-making
of my eighty-eight cerebellum

a designer spine of *morphogenetics!*
is all the knowledge I have to offer
nested, twisted, inside of trillions
little composite images of me, little blobbies
or bubbles we like to call cells
as if locking my genetics into a rounded prison
of bilipid bars
will make me forget
the way out
the way to which to return

ACKNOWLEDGEMENTS

There are numerous people in my life who have offered consistent belief in my artistic vision and practice. Without the strength and love they have generously shared with me, I would still be lost.

My mother and her partner, my sister and my grandparents have all been tremendous and continuously teach me what unconditional love is. My friendships are eclectic and help bloom dialogues that provide true happiness to my life and soul. The English and Philosophy academics at UNSW who answered my ridiculous plethora of questions and believed in my ideas have also lent significant weight to my writing.

However none of these words would even be in your hands without Joanne Fedler. Jo's deep kindness and mentorship throughout the process of publication has been astounding, and I am so thankful.

BIOGRAPHICAL NOTE

Marcus is a Poet-Artist and professional brooder currently residing on unceded Darramurragal land in Sydney, Australia.

She finished her Honours in 2021 and received The University of New South Wales' first University Medal for Creative Writing in light of her thesis investigating the relationship between fractals and poetry.

Her artwork can be found @timewobble on Instagram.

www.ingramcontent.com/pod-product-compliance
Lightning Source LLC
Chambersburg PA
CBHW030309100526
44590CB00012B/571